MY EXPERIENCE IN THE GREAT WAR

Eddie A. Sanders

Edited by Donald K. Sanders

Copyright ©-2019 Donald K. Sanders

All rights reserved.

ISBN-13: 9781793955463

DEDICATION

This is my grandfather's diary. It begins on the day he joined the Army in 1917 and ends in 1920 upon his release from service. As editor I tried to keep any changes to a minimum. This book is dedicated to all of the soldiers of the Sanders Family, of which there are many.
Donald K. Sanders

MY EXPERIENCE IN THE GREAT WAR

TENNESSEE 1917

In 1917, feeling like many others that it was only a matter of time that would see America in the midst of the Great World conflict which was at that time in full sway in Europe. All that I knew of this great conflict was that the French and the English was on one side and the Germans on the other. Apparently the war had come to a standoff and each side dug into trenches opposite each other that stretched for miles and miles. At times one side would attack the other but for months and months neither side has gained any ground at all.

I come from a fighting family just like every other family that lives in this little valley that lies at the Tennessee end of the Cumberland Gap. My fiancé's Great Granddad and his brothers came down from Philadelphia, Boston, and New York because the Tennessee Valley was the place to get a piece of land that was worth getting. It was way back in 1793 when Granddad Clouse settled in a spot called Greasy Cove. They called it Greasy Cove because there was always so much bear fat in the water. They say there was a lot of trouble with the Indians during those times.

EDDIE A SANDERS

My kin has always been soldiers; at least the men were. There was at least one Sanders and one Clouse in every war ever fought in this country and I have accepted the fact that it is my turn to pick up where my kin left off so it wasn't long before I was in line with the rest of the boys I went to school with. When we got out of that line we were all soldiers in the Army of these United States. I do not regret it as we have got to fight to protect our country and I know that you would not want a slacker. I hope someday that I will have a farm for I love the green grass and trees and animals.

They let me go back home to tell all my kin goodbye. That was a lot harder than I could have ever imagined it would be and it was a hundred times worse than that to say goodbye to my true love, Audrey. She was a Clouse through and through. She offered me her Granddad's rifle gun that she had inherited from him when he died a few weeks back. It was a fine hunting gun and I'd love to take it but everybody said that the Army would be furnishing us our shooting instruments.

After a whole lot of kissing and hugging I was off walking down the road and into town to catch the train. Audrey walked part of the way with me and the whole way she talked about how she wished she could go to the Army too. We figured that by the time we got to France the darn war would be over anyway. As a matter of fact I didn't think we would even make it to France before it was all over and we would have to turn right around and come back home after we turned in our new rifles. I don't think they would let us keep them because they were sure to have another war right after this one. We were having such a good time walking and talking that I almost missed the train when it began whistling and huffing and puffing. I gave Audrey another real quick smooch and I was off running to catch that train before missed it and the whole darn war. She waved at me and threw me kisses until I could see her no more, off in the distant. I got a empty feeling in my heart at that time and it stayed with me all those long months I was to be in France.

The first thing I found out was that there is a whole lot of yelling going on inside those Army camps. Instead of talking there was yelling and instead of walking there was running. In the morning we had to get up at the normal time of 4:30 AM and then we would run to get in line, run to get to the mess hall, and then we had to run everywhere else all day long. I've been a runner all my life so it didn't bother me at all.

The Army was in a hurry to get us where we needed to be because there was a Master Sargent yelling at us to get into a line and nobody knew where the line was going so we waited in one line that led us to another line and so on and so forth, for days and days. That Sargent yelled at us for everything. It was, "Turn left, turn right, shut up, get in line", and then it was, "Get on the train!" I didn't say anything but that guy sure was giving me a headache.

If you think we were comfortable on that train you better think again. There were no passenger cars on this train because all they had was boxcars. They had us all squished up and sitting on the floor. The bad thing about it was that we all had beans for chow and the odor in that car was not pleasant at all. One after another we took turns peeing out the rolling door and if you pointed the wrong way it came right back in on us.

About the time we got settled in on the train we were at our destination. I had never been more than 50 miles from home so I didn't know where the heck we were and I couldn't tell you how to get there either.

We got off the train at Camp Forrest on the border of Tennessee and Georgia. The Sargent yelled at us to get up and off the darn train but my legs were asleep from sitting so long in the cramped up train. I didn't jump off the train, I fell off and almost landed on top of that yelling Sargent. He wanted to know if I thought that was funny and was I a wise guy. I don't know what he was yelling about but after about a half hour he pointed us in the direction to where we would begin out training as soldiers.

Camp Forrest was named for General Nathan Bedford Forrest of Civil War fame. Forrest was the hero of the battle at Chickamauga and he was considered to be the best of the Confederate Generals. It was often said that if everyone would have gotten out of his way he could have won the war. After the war he became the head of the KKK.

We were at this camp only a couple of weeks and it was getting cold because winter was setting in on us. On February 22, 1917 I found myself on the train again leaving Camp Forrest in Oglethorpe Georgia heading to San Benito, Texas for some advanced training. It was on this train that I met and befriended three brothers, Jimmy, John, and JB Norris, all of Eastern Tennessee which was the Confederate side of the state which explains why they were sitting with all those Arkansas

MY EXPERIENCE IN THE GREAT WAR

boys and farting and telling jokes. These boys had me laughing from the moment we met and I was to laugh with them almost until the war's end.

We were assigned to the 26th Infantry at this place. It was with this organization that we received our first day of advanced training as soldiers. The first thing we were taught was squad formation drills, marching drills and physical training. Thanks to the antics of JB Norris our whole platoon was in excellent shape having to do thousands of extra pushups every time he got us into trouble. I would always get caught laughing at his loud stinky farts and the Sargent always thought I was the one doing all the farting. I just couldn't help myself. Within a couple of days we were assigned to our respective companies. The four of us was sent to Company K out of Corpus Christi, Texas, a small city on the Gulf Coast. I guess the Norris brothers were sent with us Yankees because they wanted to keep all the farters in one bunch. While we were at this place war was declared against Germany, I never found out why.

A few weeks later we were moved to Kingsville Texas, a few miles further south along the Mexican border. Large populations of Mexicans lined all the roads and parks and I'm told that the reason for them to be here was that there was a violent revolution just a few miles across the border. The Mexican Poncho Villa often raided this area killing men, women, and children before scurrying back across the border. It seems fitting that we were taught how to use weapons at this place.

We were still on the target range when we were told that we were being shipped back to San Benito so I guess our training days were over just when they had begun. We quickly assembled and gathered our gear and moved out that same day in June 1917. Upon arrival we were told not to pitch our tents for we would be moving again very soon. We were ordered to turn in all of our warm weather gear and then we were issued winter clothing. I thought it funny that we would get winter uniforms during the summer but rumor had it we were headed for France where the summers are colder.

Everyone was unusually quiet that night and after sleeping on the ground that night when morning came we sat in the summer sun for hours until we were loaded on to a train amid cheers from the crowds in the station we were soon on our way to an unknown destination. Leaving the State of Texas far behind, we crossed into Arkansas and then on to Missouri, Illinois, Ohio, Pennsylvania, New York and New Jersey. We passed through the cities of Houston, Texarkana, Little Rock, St. Louis, Indianapolis, Springfield (Ohio), Pittsburg, Philadelphia, and Jersey City. We were traveling under "sealed orders" and very few people along the way guessed that the first American troops were on their way to take part in the fight on the Western front.

In Pittsburg it was so strongly felt that such was the case that it seemed as though they would tear up the city for when we pulled into the railroad yard whistles began to blow and the people began making such noise that we were glad when our train pulled out again just to get some peace.

Arriving in the railroad yard of Jersey City, N. J. on June 8th we were told that we would live on the train for the present but we were permitted to go to town on short leave of absence. Most of us took advantage of this privilege after such a long journey on the train. The four of us found a place that served bean soup and pickled eggs. We made sure to eat our fill of this knowing full well what was going to happen. On the way back to the train we all stopped and bought a package of those new cigarettes that everyone was talking about. The salesman asked where we were bound but we didn't say a word and just walked out. We were not allowed to talk to anyone along the way to the boats for evident reasons. Early on the morning of June 10th our train pulled out again and we were soon unloading at the ferry where we crossed to Hoboken N. J.

It was there that the beans and pickled eggs began to work their magic. When they opened the doors to the train the boys were fighting to get out first to escape the stink of our pickled boiled eggs that filled the inside of the RR car. To make matters worse we all got sick from smoking those damn cigarettes. I have to say that we were not real popular with the rest of the boys. I guess that if we were on fire, none of those boys would even pee on us.

We marched while letting loose with the loudest farts ever heard in the quiet streets of Hoboken and the whole company was laughing and having a hell of a good time. In just a short time we found ourselves at the pier where the small transport ship Momus awaited us. Once we were aboard her we became what was to be the very first convoy of American troops headed towards the war. We were accompanied by the transport ships the

Henderson, the Antilles, and the Lenape, all full of American soldiers. Months later we heard that the Antilles was sunk by an enemy torpedo on its return trip with a heavy loss of life.

Going aboard immediately we began to settle ourselves for the long trip ahead of us. We moved out into the outer harbor on June 10th and before daylight on June 14th we sailed out from New York Harbor. Most of us found ourselves seasick as soon as we cleared the harbor. We were paying dearly for eating those beans and eggs and I guess we deserved the ill treatment we got from the rest of the company just for a little stinky belly gas.

We were instructed in boat drill and given our positions in case it became necessary to abandon ship. It was required that we wear our life preservers at all times. No lights were allowed and no trash was to be thrown overboard.

There were four 6 inch guns on the ship, In Navy lingo there was two afore and two aft. During the daytime these same guns were frequently used for target practice. The targets were let out on a long line behind the "Submarine Chasers" that accompanied us across. On most of the voyage we changed course frequently running in a zigzag manner.

We each had to do our share of guard duty and were especially instructed to watch out for submarines when on guard on the deck. No submarines were sighted however but four days before we landed one was reported near us and the naval boats were sure busy for a while dropping depth bombs, etc.

MY EXPERIENCE IN THE GREAT WAR

Three days before we landed French boats met us and accompanied us on the rest of the trip. They were very small in comparison to our own naval escort. On June 25th we sighted land and on the next day we pulled into the port of St. Nazaine, France.

.

MY EXPERIENCE IN THE GREAT WAR

FRANCE

I was lucky enough to get assigned to a small detail of eight men who went ashore on June 26th to prepare for the rest of our company to come ashore the next day. My friends Willis S. Carter, James Choate, and Thomas J. Evans and the Norris brothers were with me as we went off marching through the streets like we owned the place. Farther out down the road we came to the camp which was about a mile from the town. We found that the French girls walking along the road were very, very friendly and we were all considering going absent without leave. There were several German prisoners busy working on the buildings that were still under construction. It was hardly a camp yet for there was only the hastily built "cantonments." Spending the night there we depended on our own equipment and supplies we had brought with us on the boats.

Late the next morning the rest of the regiment came marching down the road to join us. The very next morning we began our training in St. Nazaine by taking a long hike to the beach where we drilled all day in the hot June sun, returning late in the evening to camp where we were required to stay, not being allowed to leave because of a couple of cases of Meningitis in our regiments. This is what we were told anyway but rumor has it that there was an epidemic of venereal disease running rapid among the regiment.

We continued our routine hikes and drills here until the 21st of July when we broke camp and marched to waiting trains where we were crowded into box cars again to begin a two day journey across the central part of France. Sleep was next to impossible due to our crowded conditions.

Arriving in Demange France which was my company's destination we were assigned to "billets" which were stables, barns, lofts, etc, where we slept on straw spread on the floor or on field cots that some of us had with us. The place assigned to the squad I belonged to was in the loft of an old harness making shop.

Our training in this new village now began in earnest. We soon became accustomed to hearing first call at three and four in the morning when we would get out, eat a hastily prepared breakfast, and upon receiving our usual corn beef sandwich and French bread we would be on our way, rain or shine to the drill grounds some 15 kilometers away. Here we received instruction from French soldiers who were sent there for that purpose. After a full day of drills and instruction we returned to our billets exhausted and hungry. The next day would find us up and ready for even harder tasks then the day

before. It was well that we maintained such a spirit for we soon found that with the cold weather we would look back at the summer with regret for the cold and rainy weather did not halt our training in the least.
Our first payday since leaving the States was received while stationed in this town. Our time was pretty well taken up and we hardly had time to buy anything from the few French stores about the place. Some of the men took a day or two absence and went to the larger towns located in our area. Upon returning from such trips they had to serve short periods in the guard house as a result. As further punishment they were made to perform such tasks as raking the mud from the streets of the town, digging trenches in the local drill grounds at night besides going out to drill in the daytime with their regular companies.
We were frequently inspected by the General Staff of our own command and by officers of the French and English often standing for hours with full packs in the rain waiting for the inspecting groups to appear. This was also in addition to our regular drills.
On August 28th of 1917 Frank Pagan and Arthur Vandine, two boys from my camp, and I crept out of camp and went on a little trip on our own which carried us to Southern France. Catching a train in Demange we made our first stop in Chateau Theiny, a city close to the front which was held at that time by the French.
Arriving in this place in the night we began to look for a place to spend the rest of the night.
Leaving the railway station we walked down the main street of the town. There were no lights and we met very few people in the streets. Finally crossing a bridge to

another section of the town we found a café where e engaged a room for the night. This was the best place we could find for all the hotels were closed up. Getting up the next morning we had breakfast which consisted of eggs, butter, hot bread, and coffee. Later we had a few glasses of champagne. The meal certainly was an enjoyable one after eating the food given us in our companies.

After breakfast we decided to go on to Paris and going to the station again we caught a train for the capital city. Pagan suggested before we even left the station that we go to Dijon France and we were soon on an express train for the latter city. Here we met the first American soldiers since leaving our company. They were members of the First Engineers who were stationed here. From Dijon we went to Lyons and on to Marseilles on the South Eastern coast of France. I believe we were the first American soldiers of the A. E. F. to visit this place and the people looked upon us with curiosity. We were treated in a royal manner everywhere we went about the city. Not desiring to stay away from our company too long we made arrangements to return to our training area by the most direct area. We came back to Demange on September 2nd after being absent for 5 days.

Such trips not being legal according to Army Regulations, Captain R. K. Whitson, our company commander gave us extra duty which we accepted feeling that the trip was well worth it. Eight days later I was on a detail with the others of my squad to do some work on the recreation hut located in our town. We were marching down the street on our way to the building when a line of trucks and a detachment of teamsters on their mules came down the narrow streets going in our same direction. The mules became excited almost throwing off the rider of the one nearest us.

We scattered of course and in doing so I unknowingly backed into one of the trucks. It knocked me down and ran over my left leg. Thinking I was not badly hurt I got to my feet intending to go on with the rest of the men but after a step or two my leg gave way and I had to be carried to the first aide station a short ways on the edge of town.

The Major doctor in charge of the first aide station, after examining me, put splints on my leg and ordered me sent to a field hospital about thirty kilometers away near Neufchatel. On arriving at the hospital the doctors reset my leg and put on a plaster cast. The plaster cast was removed three weeks later and after a few more days in the hospital I requested to go back to my company. On October 10th I rejoined my outfit which was now stationed in the small town of Menucourt.

This new place where we were was about 285 kilometers from the town of Demange. The next day after coming back to my organization we went out on a long march of about 15 kilometers where the whole division assembled and passed in review for the President of France, General Pershing, and other officials. I had to fall out, having injured my leg again. Hiking back to camp I was put on sick report for a few days then returned to regular duty.

We continued our training in this, the "Gondicourt area" while the two infantry divisions in the 1st Brigade, the 16th and 18th went into the front line trenches. After they had been "in the line" for a few days a report was read to the different companies of my regiment describing a raid the Germans made upon Company E, 16th Infantry. The report stated that a barrage was put down on our men, and the German infantry attacked in force killing and capturing some of them. It stated that the enemy had surprised our sentries by the suddenness of the attack, cutting the throats of some of them. Of course this was war but the report intensified the desire on the part of the men of the 1st Division for revenge.

MY EXPERIENCE IN THE GREAT WAR

THE TRENCHES

On November 4th, 1917 my company began moving toward the front with the other organizations of the 2nd Brigade. We hiked part of the way and then loaded onto French trucks which were chauffeured by Chinese drivers. This was a great relief in that we had been used to hiking in the performance of our duties about the training areas. We arrived in Mate, a small town near Battlemont from which town this sector of the front derived its name. We remained in Mate until the 1st and second battalions of the regiment put up 10 days each on the front line. We began to hike to the trenches in the latter part of November in a cold and drizzling rain. Marching along the hard surfaced road until we came to some woods just in back of the front line trenches, here we went through muddy fields. Our long rain soaked overcoats becoming so heavy and with the heavy packs we carried it was hard to keep our feet much less march through the mud, but this was only the beginning of what was to come later. Coming to the second trenches which ran around the brow of a hill we began to relieve the company that was holding this section of the line.

MY EXPERIENCE IN THE GREAT WAR

There was a tunnel dugout running through the hill from the second to the front trenches.
We passed through this to the front line where we were assigned to our different posts. I was stationed at a post in the trench where there was a step-up from the bottom of the trench. We could stand upon this and see across no-man's-land to where the German trenches were about eighteen hundred yards across the shell torn valley. There was very little action here while we were on the line as far as the infantry was concerned but the artillery; back in the woods was busy firing a few shells into the German lines most of the time. No casualties resulted from our ten day period in the line.
After being relieved we began our hike back to the training area about Gondrecourt. Before leaving the front it was passed around that a surprise awaited us upon arriving in our respective towns. We came back to Menecourt on Saturday and the next day we were all detailed to carrying rocks and building roads about camp in the rain. After that we looked forward to any pleasant surprise. We began at this time to maneuver and drill on a larger scale. Our training had been conducted about the town where we were billeted and consisted of training in the use of hand grenades, rifle grenades, the French Chauchet rifle, bayonet drill, and gas mask drill etc. This training was confined to regimental and brigade type drill but now we began to take larger hikes and the maneuvers were of longer duration.
On one occasion we were called out about two o'clock in the morning and started a hike which brought us to

Mourage, a small town about 20 kilometers away. Arriving here we were quartered in barn lofts about town. The ground was now covered with a deep snow and the streets were slick with ice. It was so cold that we could not get warm without fires.

We were called out before daylight the next morning. Eating our meager breakfast and receiving our sandwich we were soon out for an all day sham battle. The 26th and the 28th Infantry was the attacking side and the 16th and 18th Infantry were the defending side. This performance ended up a good distance away and after being completed we had to hike back to Mourage, arriving there after dark.

There was very little protection from the weather in the place where we slept. In the place where I was quartered the roof was full of holes and the snow was all about in the building. Our shoes were soaked as were the rest of our clothing from lying down and wading in the snow. The next morning we had to thaw them out to put them on.

We continued to maneuver and drill in this area for seven more days and nights. We were often called out in the middle of the night for guard duty in the drill trenches. The rest of the night most of this was done in below 0 deg weather.

In the afternoon of the seventh day we left the drill trenches of the training center. We hiked through the now sloppy fields and down the ice covered roads back to Menecourt in a cold rain mixed with sleet. There were other organizations of the same Division going to their respective towns. After getting back to Menecourt we removed our wet overcoats and began to try to get warm.

We had hardly begun when we were called out again, this time for inspection from General Headquarters. We lined up in the street in front of our billets and the Inspecting Officer made his way up and down the lines and then made their way through our sleeping quarters. Upon entering our billet one of the Officers asked our Captain, "What are these men doing in here when they are supposed to be out standing on inspection?" Our Captain replied that those are the men's overcoats and that they were frozen and standing up so they looked like men standing there. It was rather dark in the quarters so it was an easy mistake to make.

Our training continued in this manner right on through December. When Xmass came we were expecting to get paid because on the November payday we were up at the front and missed the paymaster. We were disappointed again and so we went about our regular duties on XMass Eve but on XMass day we were excused from regular duty except for the kitchen crew and etc. They too could have taken off from duty because the meal they served was very much like a regular day's meal.

It was a silent bunch of guys that sat in the billets trying to keep warm in the well ventilated room. We shivered from the cold and even the small fires could do little toward keeping us warm. Late in the afternoon Joe Hunton, our top sergeant who always seemed to have a little money came to our quarters and loaned each of us a few Franks that we spent on wine so we set about making merry thus changing the picture of one of gloom to one of cheerfulness.

Continuing the ridged training here until the middle of January (1918) some of the organizations of the Division began to leave the Gondrecourt area for the front. The Second Infantry Brigade remained however, leaving for the front in February. We hiked all the way to the front this time. We stopped for a couple of days in Rambecourt, a small town about five kilometers in back of the front like trenches. Later we hiked across the fields to Rambecourt which was only a kilometer from the front. Coming into this place at night we were assigned to cellars and dugouts for the night. The next morning we awoke and took stock of our surroundings. The town was mostly a mass of ruins hardly a whole building in the place. The only clear road ran straight through the town.

That night we went out on a detail to raise some barb wire entanglement back up in the marshy fields a short ways. While out on this detail a gas alarm sounded. Putting on our gas masks we continued our work which was difficult enough without the discomfort. None of the men on our detail was affected by the gas however but soon after making a test to see if there was any gas in our vicinity we removed our masks. Our work could be conducted better at night under the circumstances so we had some leisure time during the day.

We witnessed some of the hardest fought battles of the air while we were here. The German planes would try to penetrate our lines and meeting our planes there would result a terrific battle. They would sometimes fight for hours with some of the planes falling to the ground in flames. We soon learned the difference between the roar of our planes and the German planes. The latter gave off an uneven roar while our planes gave an even roar. This proved valuable in identifying German planes over our lines.

The enemy artillery frequently shelled the town, roads and our own artillery battery's located along the Rambecourt and Beaumont roads, a distance of about three kilometers. On one occasion some of us were playing pinochle in an open court between two buildings facing the main street of the town when the Germans began dropping shells all about us which broke up the game.

Having come to the front for more serious business a day or two later we started for the main front line trenches. Hiking along the Rambecourt and Beaumont road a ways then we turned off to the left taking a route through the marshy fields to Sieschiprey. Entering the network of trenches here we began the relief of the company that was holding this sector about the place. In the darkness we staggered about the trench like a bunch of drunken men weighted down with our heavy equipment. As we moved in the rats were pushed out and some of them were as big as cats. Finally the relief of the other company was completed and we began an all night watch at our different posts along the trench which was more like sloughs in places the water and mud was so deep. It seemed to me that the rats were trying to communicate with us their displeasure of having to move out.

There was a constant rattle of machine gun and rifle fire all night all along the front mixed with the loud crashing of the artillery shells from the German and American batteries. Flares and signal rockets were shot up frequently lighting things up almost as light as day. We had a password to use to identify ourselves and to keep the Germans from entering our trenches to gather information. We were not permitted to have personal letters or papers on us that would give away information to the enemy in case we should be captured. When dawn came we were directed to dugouts in the main trenches that were knee deep in slimy, muddy water. My dugout had about three feet of water and wooden platforms to sleep on. We were issued boots but they didn't do very much toward keeping us dry. At night no lights or fires were permitted and we moved about the trenches as little as possible in the daytime for the Germans could view our every movement from MontSec, a high hill towering above us on the German side of the trenches.

A constant rain of high explosive and gas shells fell about us at night and added to this was the machine gun fire. All of this caused many causalities among our men. Our machine guns and artillery replied with equal vigor. After seven days in the main front line trenches about Sciesphney my company was relieved by another company and we retired to a position back of the line where we remained until a few days later. We entered the front line again about two kilometers from Bouconville, a town located in the left front of the same sector.

After two days with my company at this location I was detailed as a messenger for battalion headquarters located in Bouconville. The reserve companies of the 3rd battalion "L" and "M" was also stationed here. Our duty as messengers was to maintain contact with the companies of our battalion in the front line and with Regimental Headquarters in Rambecourt about three kilometers away. We carried messages over points along the Bouconville – Rambecourt Road that was under constant shell fire. After a few more days in this sector the Infantry of the 26th American Division came in to relieve us.

On April 1st, 1918 one of the trucks came over the road from Bouconville from back of the line, late in the afternoon and was spotted by the Germans. Shells began bursting all about it. The driver in his efforts to save the truck tried to turn it about. In so doing he became stuck in the mud. The driver realizing he could do no more ran for the cover of a shell hole. A few minutes later the truck was a mass of ruins from a direct hit by one of the shells.

As the Infantry companies came in it was our business as messengers to guide them to the positions of our different companies in the front line trenches. The relief was soon complete so we began hiking back from the front to a town called Toul. Here we were billeted about a kilometer from town.

After staying here a short while we were loaded onto troop trains and started another long trip across France. Passing through the outskirts of Paris late in the night we looked longingly at the lights of the city. Paris was not for us yet and we were soon on our way again and trying to get some much needed sleep in the overcrowded box cars.

Leaving the trains about 40 kilometers from Paris we started our cross country hike of about 70 kilometers. We stopped at all the small towns along the way until we came to Chaumont, France on the afternoon of April 8th. As usual we were billeted about the town in barns, lofts, etc. This place being a good distance from the front it was not marred by constant shellfire that the towns we had left had suffered. It was a relief to be stationed in surroundings such as this after what had happened before. We still carried evidence of our recent experiences though.

We had not received an issue of clothing in a while and the prospect of getting any looked very slim. Cooties were with us to stay it seemed and it looked like they would devour us before we could get a chance to get rid of them. This applied to our officers as well for their chances of keeping clean was very little better than the privates. We left Chaumont and hiked on to Flossy, a small town about 50 kilometers distant in the direction of the front, a few days later.

Stopping in some woods about half way to this place we pitched our small pup tents. We camped here until the next night when call-to-arms was sounded at about 12 o'clock. Having been taught the value of speed we pulled down our tents, rolled up our packs, and scrambled to the road ready to march in about 15 minutes. We hiked the rest of the night and all the next day coming into Flossy at about dusk almost exhausted from the lack of sufficient food and sleep. Our feet were so sore from the continuous hiking we could hardly walk.

It was evident that the men knew what was expected of

them and experiences of this kind were accepted in a cheerful manner. While here at this place, which was about 30 kilometers from the front we took our clothing to the de-lousing station where machines had been brought up for this purpose. When they were removed from the steaming tanks they were hardly fit to wear on dress parade.

On the 15th of May we loaded onto trucks and started for the front line to relieve other organizations of the 1st Division who had preceded us to the front. We proceeded along the road singing the different songs that were common to us at the time. The sudden roar of the guns told us that this liked a whole lot of being a quiet sector. As we grew neared it was becoming dark and we could see the continual flashing of the artillery guns.

Leaving the trucks at a safe distance we proceeded on foot to Breys. What was once a small town was now just a pile of ruins. The streets were littered with stones and bricks from the collapsed buildings. We slept in a deep, roomy dugout in the heart of town that was big enough for a whole platoon of 42 men.

The following night we moved out again going through wheat fields and a communicating trench we came to the main front line trench at a point about 2 kilometers from Brayes. As before in other sectors of the front we had occupied we relieved the company holding the line at this point. The trenches here ran off to the left and the right of a ravine which also ran back about two hundred yards. The ravine gave off to a small valley in the no-man's-land. We were distributed along both sides of this ravine and two teams of automatic riflemen of four each took up positions beyond the front line in shell holes in no-man's-land. They were close enough to the enemy to hear them talking some times. We had taken over the positions under difficult circumstances. Artillery shells, shrapnel and machine gun fire covered our trenches while making our relief and it continued throughout the night.

We set about strengthening our positions by digging new trenches and improving the shallow ones already started. This was not an easy task for the enemy machine gun bullets swept our trenches regularly. To get our outposts it was necessary to crawl along a ditch leading out into no man's land from the ravine and all access an open space where it was very easy to be spotted when a flair was shot up. A detail from my platoon had to make this trip every night to take food to the men on outpost. Raiding parties were sent out most every night and hand to hand fighting began to be a common thing. These raiding parties were usually made up from the organizations back in reserve, the companies in the front trenches cooperating with them. On the main we had control of no-man's land from the time we entered the line here. We had been fighting under the Command of French General Headquarters because we were attached to the French Army Corps. But now we held this sector on our own and orders had been issued by the American Command not to wait for the enemy to attack but to beat him to it and give him hell. Of course the French on both sides of our sector cooperated with us as we did with them. We retired from our positions in the trenches to dugouts along in the ravine a short way at dawn each morning returning to our posts at darkness again. We got what sleep and rest we could in the dug in places in the steep banks of the ravine. These holes were not very deep and in the case of my own it was a hole covered over with dirt and brush. We received the one meal in 24 hours at night. Four or five men were detailed every night to go back about a kilometer and bring up the cans containing the food. This was a dangerous mission for the field we had to cross was swept with machine gun fire and shellfire. The food was prepared at a distance back of the line and then put in the canisters which were brought up in mule carts by the kitchen crew over the shell town roads and fields through constant shell fire. On the morning of May 26th, 1918, while in this same position on the Cantigny-Montdider front Colonel Hamilton A Smith our Regimental Commander and Captain R. K. Whitson inspected our position. As a result orders were issued that information had been obtained from prisoners captured the previous night that an attack was expected at this point of our line and that we prepare to fight in place. We went at to our usual posts in the trenches on each side of the ravines at dusk the two teams of automatic riflemen going to the outposts in no-man's land.

Orders were for the men on outposts to retire to the front trenches in case of attack and take a position with the rest of our platoon. Except for the increased machine gun fire, shells and shrapnel bursting all about us the expected attack had not materialized at dawn. It was believed the attack was postponed. We in the front trench went to our dugouts and received the only food we had had since the preceding night. This consisted of a can of salmon to two men and French bread. We had barely reached our dugouts and started to eat when shells and shrapnel begin to fall thick about us which soon increased to barrage intensity. We rushed from our dugouts to the trenches Lt. Oral, our platoon Commander, shouting directions to us. This was hardly necessary for we knew from passed training and experience what to do. We took our positions in the shallow trenches a few feet apart, constantly watching for the enemy to appear though the dense smoke clouds produce by the barrage. The general bombardment lasted about three hours then changed to a lot barrage. We begin to see the columns of German infantry coming over the shell-torn fields of no-man's land at the intervals through the clouds of smoke and bursting shells. This started the small arms fire from our own men. They kept on coming to our outposts they resisting to the very last man as they retired toward the front line trench. Later it developed that only one man from the outposts escaped being killed or wounded. The Germans came to within a few feet of our trench but meeting with such resistance they soon begin to retreat to their own line, leaving many of their men killed and wounded behind. The shelling of our trenches continued but with much less intensity and we could see a greater distance than when the barrage was at its worst. The fields about was littered with smoking shell holes, the grass burning from the hot fragments of high explosive shells. The men of my platoon assembled near the ravine and upon checking our losses we found we had lost twenty men having had 112 men upon entering the line our Lieutenant was among those wounded. We could not take the killed and wounded back that day. We gave the wounded what first aide we could and those that could walked back to the first aide stations. The men I especially remember as getting killed in this attack was Nicholas Schnider and William Kellish. Schnider was killed by a direct hit by a shell which hit him in the chest. Kellish being killed by the explosion of a German hand grenade which exploded close to his face taking away his whole face. That night I helped take these two men back to a road about a kilometer where we left them for the burial detail. Taking the cans of "chow" that the kitchen crew had brought up near this point we returned to the front line. The next day, as was planned, the 28th and first battalion of the 26th infantry was ordered to hold what we had. Remaining in our same position we witnessed the attack. The lines of advancing infantry could be seen deployed in attack formation going at a regular gait behind the French tanks. Some of the men could be seen falling out when killed or wounded. But the others never stopped. Aeroplanes were flying low and lead directing the artillery which was putting down a rolling barrage in front of the advancing infantry. In our eagerness to watch this, the first offensive advance of the American Expeditionary Forces in France, we forgot about the shells falling about us. Cantigny was captured and held against all counter attacks. But many of our men had been killed and wounded.

A day or two later my company was relieved from the front line. Starting back from the line in the night we hiked back toward Brays where we had spent one night on coming into this sector. On the way a gas alarm sounded nearby. We put on our gas masks and continued on stumbling over the shell torn roads and wheat fields to a point about four hundred yards from Brays, where our company head-quarters on P.C. was located. The rest of the company was distributed about in dugouts along a road leading out from Brays in the direction of the front line.

We were now in Regimental reserve but still within easy reach of the enemy artillery. The reserve trenches ran across a hill in back of our dugouts. Artillery gun positions scattered along the road between our position and the town, dug into the high bank along the road and were covered over with camouflage to hide them from the eyes of the enemy airplanes and observation balloons. They were often discovered and heavy shilling of the position resulted. The town of Braye was a constant target and from our elevated position we could see the shells pour into the place, the brick stone and roof tile flying hundreds of feet in the air and falling all about the place.

Replacements were received at this time to take the place of the men we had lost on this front. We envied them their clean looking uniforms at having been so long since we had received an issue of clothing that the ones we had were torn and dirty from crawling about in them. Their clothes were soon as bad as our own. Alvin Schroder, a Corporal in my company, and I were sitting under a tree overlooking the town and the gun positions scattered about the place.

We could see some of the doughboys sitting about in the

shade of the trees near town. A German airoplane appeared above us. It circled about a few times then headed back to his own lines, shells from our anti-aircraft guns bursting all about him but with very little effect. A short while later shell began to fall among the men below us under the trees. They began to run for the cover of their dugouts through the bursting shells and clouds of smoke. Most of them seemed to reach cover safely but one of them was running along a fence, the shells hitting a few feet from him as he ran. Finally one hit almost under him and it seemed to us that it got him. But when the smoke of the shell cleared away we saw him making for safety again seemingly unhurt.

We were on many details while we were located in this reserve position, digging trenches and taking supplies up to the men on the front line. On one action my platoon furnished a detail to carry ammunition for a raiding party that was to go over from the sector of the front line my platoon had previously held. Going almost in a run, we went through the wheat fields to a communicating trench and then followed this to some woods about two kilometers distant. Reaching these woods we each took a box of trench mortar detonators and started back over the same route we had come, staggering along through the narrow trenches with heavy boxes. As we came nearer our destination in the front line, shells began to fall about us causing us to drop the boxes and fall to the ground to escape the flying fragments of shells. Coming to the front line and putting down our loads we either fell or lay down upon the ground exhausted. The raiding party was in readiness and in a few minutes started out on its grim mission across no-man's-land.

It was at this time that I was knocked off my feet. I don't think I was unconscious; maybe I was in shock. There was a loud ringing in my ears and I wobbled a bit when I tried to stand up. Both of my arms were red but I was so dazed that I had no idea why. Someone was shaking me roughly and his face was inches from my face. His lips were moving like he was yelling at me but I couldn't hear anything but the ringing in my ears. I tried to walk but someone tripped me and I fell on top of him. I thought about yelling at him for a moment until it dawned on me that we had been hit by the German artillery.

Someone was wiping my face with a cloth and when I tried to see who I had tripped on he pulled my face around the other way. I realized my hands were red because they were covered with blood. I thought I must have been wounded but I didn't know where I had been hit. Now I knew I could hear again because the person wiping my face kept saying, "you are all right, you are all right!" If it wasn't my blood on my hands and arms, whose was it?

I found I was sitting on some one's foot so I turned to see whose foot it was. I could not believe what I was looking at and I realized I was screaming in disbelief! The leg belonged to Jimmy Norris. He was obviously dead and beside him laid his two brothers John and JB. All three were looking at me as if they wanted to say something but they could not because they were dead. They lay together in a tight group like they were in a football huddle. I began to cry and I didn't stop for I don't know how long. I thought I would cry forever. From that day to this I was in a heavy daze, living in a dark fog and everywhere I looked there was death. Someone pulled me away from the Norris brothers and that was the last I saw of my three friends. I was led back to our own position in the reserve line. We got back there just before daylight. Things were happening in fast order on this front and experiences such as this were common to most of the organizations of the First Division. We could hear the thunderous roar of artillery firing off to our right where a terrific battle seemed to be in progress. Orders were issued at this time that a general advance against our section was expected and as before, we were to prepare to fight in place. About eleven o'clock on the night of June 8th a heavy barrage was put down upon us and I was beset with fear. We took up our positions in the reserve trenches, the shells bursting all about us. We were on the alert for the expected attack which seemingly had begun. Shortly after going to our posts in the trench the smell of gas was noticed and a general gas alarm was sounded. We put on our gas masks and continued at our posts until early in the morning we went to our dugouts a few yards away. On the way to the dugouts I was peppered with fragments and my gas mask canister was punctured by a piece of shell making it useless. Some of the men had to take off their masks in order to get a breath of air. Entering our dugouts we put blankets over the entrance in our efforts to keep the gas out. But the air was already saturated with both the mustard and chlorine kind from the many shells that burst about our position.

The expected attack had not come at daylight but much damage had been done in both the infantry and artillery and many had been killed, wounded and gassed. There was thirty-five of my company gassed at one time by a shell that penetrated our dugouts. This number included two of our officers. I became deathly sick from inhaling the fumes of gas and standing in front of our dugout I began to vomit. I had been slightly gassed before and I didn't think I had gotten so much of it in my system. I thought I was sure to drown in my own vomit. Lieutenant Bayard Brown thought different however for when he came up to me he told me that I was gassed and to go back to the first aide station back in Brays. We started back through the wheat fields. I came upon a battalion of artillerymen who had moved into position since the night before. They began to laugh as I approached. Looking down at my clothes I could see they were torn and dirty I realized what a spectacle I made. The crotch of my uniform was wide open to the world.

They sat me down and gave me a cup of coffee before I continued on to Brays and the first aide station vomiting up the coffee on the way. I joined the line entering the first aide station where I waited my turn for treatment. There were many other men both gassed and wounded waiting. My eyes and nose were smarting and it seemed like I would throw up my whole insides. The doctor had me wash my face with laundry soap and water and he put some medicine in my eyes that increased the burning. He told me to sit down and wait for an ambulance that was due in a few minutes. The ambulance came shortly and after as many of us loaded in that could. I thanked God when we pulled out, headed to the rear of the line.

We stopped for a few minutes at an evacuation hospital where they gave us some hot chocolate which we (the ones that were gassed) immediately vomited up again. We stopped again at an American field hospital where all of our clothes except shoes were taken away from us on account of them being so full of gas. They gave us pajamas to wear and more hot drinks which made us awful sick. I vomited up some of the greenest stuff I ever saw. Upon taking a bath here the burning about my body increased. Some of us were loaded into an ambulance again and along in the night we came to a French gas hospital near Grandville France.

I found many men here from my own company who had preceded me here during the day from the front. I could hardly see or talk and eating became a thing to be dreaded. They only fed us liquid food while here. I stayed here in the hospital five days. At the end of this period we were given a mixture of French, English and America clothes, most of them having been worn and laundered. My uniform consisted of a deep blue French coat much too small for me, a pair of almost white britches too large, a pair of English square toed shoes, American leggings and overseas cap. The bunch of us looked like we had started to a tacky party.

On June 14th, after staying five days, we boarded an American hospital train, started on another long trip, to the western coast of France. We stopped one night in the city of Rennes then proceeded on, the next day arriving in Savaney, a small town not far from St. Nazaine where we had landed a year before. Going from the depot to the hospital (American base hospital #8) in trucks we began to unload when the American doughboys questioned our right to admittance they thinking we were Frenchmen because of our semi-French uniforms. After finding out for sure that we really were Americans, we were soon assigned to wards in the hospital. Many of the men were being sent back to the "States" from this place on account of wounds received at the front. I remained here for treatment until the 3rd of August (1918) when I went before a board of doctors for examination. They told me that due to my physical condition I had been classified as Class B according to hospital classification. I understood this to mean that I was soon on the slow tedious trip which would eventually bring me back to my company. I passed through the Casual Camp at St. Agnan where I stopped four days, just long enough to secure the necessary clothing and equipment.

Upon receiving a complete uniform, I again loaded a troop train with many other casuals returning to duty from the hospitals and we were soon within the vicinity of the front. We changed from standard gauged railroad to one of arrow gauge not very far from the city of Nancy. The engines and cars were small them being used mostly to haul ammunition and supplies to the troupes at the front. We passed through the outskirts of Nancy late in the evening of August 14th. This city was being shelled by long range guns and bombed by aeroplanes. It began to grow dark and the French brakeman of our dinky train with his lantern put open was going about the train. The American doughboys made him put the light out for we well knew that lights were taboo here with the aeroplanes flying about overhead.

Leaving the train we hiked on toward the front line. As we came nearer those whom I had been traveling with from the Casual Camp began to search for their own companies of the First Division which was in the front line near Port-A-Mousson. I hiked on with those of my own organization. We passed through the small, almost deserted, towns of Griscount, Jezainville, and along a main road to a much larger place which we found to be Port-A-Mousson. We met an American sentry in the town, which seemed otherwise deserted, who told us our company was back west of this place and that we were too close to the front trenches to be moving about in the daytime.

We went across the fields to our company located on a steep hillside in the woods overlooking the town of Port-A-Mousson. This was a support line, in the trenches run around the steep hillsides. Having been away from my company since June 9th and this was August 15th, I had not heard very much from them or of their activities. But I now learned of the hard fighting the "outfit" had experienced on the Soissons front where they had, after leaving the front, advanced on July 18th, 1918. They had come out of the line with only thirty-five men with a sergeant left in command. The outfit had been sent to this quiet section for a rest. It sure did need it for we had been regularly on the go for a long time. There were raiding and aeroplane attacks upon our section here however resulting in many casualties.

From our high position on the hill we could see a great deal of the surrounding country. The town of Pont-Mousson, below us surrounded by green fields and wooded hills. In the warm summer sun this scene looked so peaceful that it was hard to believe that a deathly struggle was taking place. Such peaceful thoughts were frequently interrupted by the shells falling and bursting about over the woods and the rattle of machine guns up and down the front. Toward the latter part of our stay here there was increased artillery firing at a distance to the left of our section and we were soon to head in that direction.

We received replacements here and during the night of August 23rd - 24th we were relieved by men of the 90th American Division. The shelling of trenches and woods about our position caused some speculation as to whether an attack was about to be made here. Relief was successfully completed however and we moved back of the line, loaded into trucks and we were soon back in the vicinity of our original training area near Gondrecount. Here we were billeted about in the small towns. After two weeks of intensive drill and maneuvers we started back to the front again which was about 70 kilometers away. We moved a part of the way in trucks eventually coming to the same section of the front we had held in the spring. The division was camped in the woods a short distance from the familiar towns of Rambecourt and Beaumont.

The woods were thick with American troops and the roads thick with artillery, ammunition and supply trucks, machine gun carts, and rolling kitchens, all trying to get over the almost impassable roads. It was raining most of the time now and our clothes were constantly wet and muddy. Orders were issued for us to enter the front line and on the night of September 11th we began moving toward our position in a hard rain. We hiked along a narrow gauge railroad track through the woods, then on through the muddy fields. Coming to Beaumont we passed around it taking over a position held by a company of the 167th Infantry 42nd Division. The front line trench here was half full of water from the heavy rain and we deployed in battle formation in front of it. A few minutes later the Germans sent up some flares and began shelling us firing point blank at our line. Some of our men went down either killed or wounded, it was hard to tell in the inky darkness. We dropped into the trench, the water coming to our waists. The Germans before us seemed to sense that something unusual was about to take place here for he continued to shoot up flares, and shell our trenches and artillery positions. Some of our artillery had moved up to our own front line but in order not to let the enemy guess our intentions they fired the usual number of shells. Our platoon commander standing in the trench beside me became sick but wouldn't listen to going back to a first aid station. He was later shot through the muscle of the leg but still continued on with us over the top. About one o'clock there seemed to be a lull in the activity along the front, then the long-range guns began firing back of us. This seemed to be a signal to the rest of our artillery. For it seemed as though every gun was turned loose at once, the resulting flashes making it almost light as day.

EDDIE A SANDERS

.

OVER THE TOP

  The ground was in a quiver from the bombardment they were putting down upon the enemy. The flares were sent up one after another from his lines watching for the advance that he was sure would come. The thunderous roar of the guns continued on through the night with unbelievable regularity while we waited in the trenches for the zero hour when the word would be given, "over the top."
The rain had stopped when the lights of dawn began to break, through the mist and smoke. At 5 o'clock the order was given over the top. Climbing upon the parapet of the trenches we formed in line in the first wave. It was such an ordeal to get out of the water and mud in the trenches that the men began to holler and yell thinking not at all of the fact that some of them were going over the top for their last time.
 I was a loader for an automatic rifle team of which a man George Loer was gunner and a new man in my company by the name of Padget was the clip loader. The messkit containing clips and shells for the automatic

rifle in addition to our Springfield rifles and one hundred rounds of ammunition for it, two hand grenades, two rifle grenades and our emergency packs. The packs contained four boxes of hardtack, a can of corned beef, messkit and etc. As we deployed in battle formation, five paces apart, we began to advance across no-man's-land. Soon we came to our own barbed wire entanglement. Passing through the gaps that had been cut through this, we formed in an almost perfect line. Padget the clip loader for our automatic rifle team was knocked out as we passed through the wire entanglement. We advanced on through the fog of the early morning and smoke from the shells. Those in the first wave were not supposed to stop to render first aide nor to attend to the captured German prisoners. That was the business of the many advancing waves of doughboys behind us.

About four hundred yards from our "jumping off" line we came to a stream where the enemy had established machine gun "nests" along on both banks. Going down the steep bank we attacked these as we went along the stream. Finding no other means to cross to the other side we plunged into the cold water which came up to our chins. Reaching the other bank we were prevented from crawling out by the German machine guns firing at us from points about over a hill in front of us. Bullets were splashing in the water all about us. While still partly in the water we set up our automatic rifle on the edge of the bank and fired from this position at the little puffs of smoke that marked the German gunner positions. We came out of the stream and forming with the rest of our company in the first wave.

We continued to advance up the hill over the German machine gun nests, the gunners having been cleaned out. Those that had not been killed were taken prisoner and sent back through the advancing doughboys. After reaching the top of the hill we stopped for a few minutes, this being our first objective. We began to "dig in" in preparation for a counter attack if one should come.

None came however and as soon as the wall of bursting shells, our artillery put down in front of us, began moving forward the lines of infantry started for the Germans second line of resistance that lay a few hundred yards in front of us. Paths were cut through his wire entanglement that was encountered in front of his trenches on the hill in front of us. We started, single file, through these gaps of enemy artillery and one pounders firing "point blank" at us from the trenches.

One of his guns was firing at the wire gap through which we were passing but his shots were falling short. Believing he would soon get the range on us we were rushing through the wire where we were supposed to deploy about five paces apart again. I was near the head of the column and when I came out of the gap I moved over to the right continuing on. I don't know if it was luck or not but in so doing I was out of the line of fire intended for our column, A shell burst right in the midst of the men who were still in the gap, tearing away one of Alvin Schneider's legs, a corporal in my company, and wounding some of the others.

Continuing on through increasing machine gun and rifle fire and artillery fire we came to within a few yards of the enemy's second line. They didn't seem to want to give up their position but it didn't take long to change their minds. There was a machine gun right in front of my platoon that was peppering the ground about us where we were firing from a prone position and from shell holes.

George Loer, automatic rifleman for whom I was leader, could not see the "nest" that was holding up our advance temporarily. By crawling slightly to the right I

could see the blue puffs of smoke from the gun. I pointed it out to Loer but he could not get a line on it from the prone position and the eighteen shot rifles were not so easy to fire from the shoulder standing up. He stood up however and I had to brace him at the same time putting the clips in the gun. A few minutes later orders were issued to attack but this was not necessary for the men were running out ahead of the line firing as they went.
As we came closer to the trenches the Germans that had not been killed by our artillery, machine guns, and rifle fire, came out with their hands up. One old German, in the excitement, forgot to remove his belt that contained his side arms and came over to our trench with his hands out instead of up. I had started on toward the trench when I saw him. I came back to him and with my rifle and bayonet at "short jab" I was about to let him have it when I saw our Captain come in front of him and put his pistol in his chest. I jerked the German's belt off leaving him to the Captain.
There had been about twenty-seven prisoners captured here besides the many killed and wounded about in the trenches. I saw one German who was killed sitting down in the trench, his rifle in his hands and a pipe in his mouth. Most of the ones who had operated machine guns were killed. We had also suffered some casualties in this scrap. At one time a piece of shell hit my gas mask but it came from my right and only cut through my mask and buried itself in the ground beside me. This was only one of many times I almost got mine.
We advanced on through the open fields the lines of American infantry extending as far to the right as we could see and to some woods about a kilometer to our left. Many of our men were falling from the shells and bullets from the German guns in the woods but the

advance continued steadily on. Just before we reached our third objective, a hill overlooking the small town of Monsard slightly to our left, we advanced too close to our own barrage causing us to drop back a ways until our barrage began to move on again.

We were in single file. I saw a German shell explode in midst of a column of doughboys off to our left killing or wounding most of them. We stopped at the foot of the hill and turning about we continued to advance to our third objective on top of the hill where we dug in or dropped about in shell holes. Here the First Battalion of the 26th Infantry passed through our, the third battalion, ranks advancing now as the front wave. The third followed in support.

The tanks were now taking part. They attacked with the infantry going across toward Mousard where the enemy was putting up a strong resistance. We passed to the right of this place it being in the line of attack of the regiment on our left. Coming to the edge of a big woods, at dark we established a line and again prepared for a counter attack. We remained in this position until daylight the next morning (Sept. 13th) when we started over the top again taking a position in the first wave. During the night the Germans that had not been caught in our artillery barrage, .had opportunity to move out of the woods. Therefore when we began to advance through the woods little resistance was met with. We came to a narrow gauge railroad which we followed along for a short distance until we came to a road leading off to our left. A squad of men was sent to explore this and soon came back with three German rolling kitchens.

The Hun drivers were bringing food for their troops, unaware that their men had abandoned their regular positions in the trenches. We took charge of it instead and after some debate as to whether it was safe to eat we finally decided it was. We each received a share. We

didn't stay here long but continued on through the dense woods.
We came upon a railroad about which was stacked great piles of all kinds of ammunition and a short distance from this was a field hospital. We explored the deserted buildings as we passed and soon came out into open field where we could see a greater distance.
There was a small town just in front of us and to our left was another town nestling at the foot of a high hill. An ammunition dump was a fire near the batten place. When it blew, the explosion of the shells could be heard for quite a distance and great clouds of smoke rolled up from the blast. We advanced to within two hundred yards of the small village nearest us and began to dig foxholes in the open field.
I was part of a detail sent down to explore the small village which seemed deserted. We were careful to watch for possible machine gun or rifle fire. No resistance was met with however and we were soon on the streets. We found no one in the place except an old Frenchman and his wife, who seemingly had lived here among the Germans under constant shell fire.
They greeted us with tears in their eyes. We found here many artillery guns the Germans had left behind in their hasty retreat. They had plugged the guns or otherwise made them useless. Reporting back to our company we began to move further to the right finally taking up a position in a small scape of woods, establishing ourselves in this one final objective. We remained here until late in the evening of the 13th when we were relieved by other American troops and began hiking back over the same ground that had been taken from the Germans by the First Division. We hiked over the shell-torn roads to a vast wood about four kilometers away where we pitched our "pup" tents on the muddy

ground.

On the way back I had begun to feel sick having to fall out every few minutes to vomit. I had kept up with my company however and thought I would feel better when we could get some hot food which was soon brought to us by our kitchen crew. We lay down in our "pup" tents that night and slept for the first time since Sept. 11th the day before the drive began. The next morning we were up early and set about to clean up and to see what the Germans had left behind.

There were many wooden barracks where they had lived that had many things in them that surprised us. Some of them were fitted out in fine style. One even had a piano which some of the doughboys enjoyed very much. Concrete "pill" boxes all about through the woods from which they had fired the thousands of rounds of ammunition into our ranks the two preceding days and nights. But now the guns were silenced and many of the gunners were laying all about. At one place there was an anti-aircraft gun with the gun crew and horses laying about dead.

We were still in the range of the enemy artillery and shells frequently fell in the woods about us, and aeroplane fighting was a common occurrence, especially at night. The bullets from the fighting planes would bury up in the ground all about our tents. At the end of five days, on Sept. 18th we rolled up our packs and began hiking further back of the front line. Passing over the muddy roads early in the night we came to the small town of Mont-Sec located on a high hill by the same name. There wasn't any town to speak of just the shell of buildings was all that remained.

The older men of my company looked upon this place with curiosity for we had previously been in trenches in front of this place. Leaving here we went on across what had been no-man's-land into trucks and immediately began to move along the front. After riding the greater part of the night in the trucks and started toward a different section of the front line. It was raining most of the time on this hike and we could hardly keep our feet hiking in the darkness through the deep mud. We continued to gradually move on toward the front, stopping in the daytime in the woods or old camps along the way.

We eventually came to where the 28th America Division had started over the top. Here we had to leave the shell-torn roads and hike through the fields and woods. It became almost impossible for me to keep up with my organization. I had not eaten but very little since leaving the St-Michel front. But as many of the men were doing I continued on with my company.

Late in the night of Sept. 30th we came to the small town of Sheppy. The roar of the guns was constantly heard which indicated that the American divisions who were in the line were putting up a good fight. The dead, both men and horses, lying about was evidence that the ground we were passing over was won at a great cost. Orders had been issued that we would relieve the 28th American Division and would start over the top the next morning, October 1st. But it developed that our artillery had not been able to get into position by this time due to the congested traffic on the almost impassable roads. We marched on into Sheppy with the shells falling all about. When we were on the streets of this place a gas alarm sounded making it necessary for us to put on our masks. This almost knocked me out for by now I had a burning fever, my throat and lips were almost parched. We took up a battle position, a short ways from the town, on a high hill about eleven o'clock. We deployed in battle formation; digging in we prepared to attack at dawn. But as before stated, our artillery had not reached its position and orders were issued that we would attack at dawn on October 4th instead. The next evening our rolling kitchens came up in the valley in back of us. We went down the steep hill a squad at a time to eat. But the thought of food was far from my mind.

I went down with my squad however and tried to eat, but it was no use. I could not swallow the food. I gave my mess kit of steak, potatoes and gravy to one of my squad. When the others of my squad were done eating we started back up the hill. They soon left me behind for I was too weak to keep up with them. My corporal came back and helped me up the hill and told me to report to Lieutenant Brown, our Platoon Commander, and to tell him I was sick. I had not done this when soon after dark the corporal and the lieutenant came to the shell hole where I was at. The lieutenant told me to go back to a first aid station a short distance down in the valley.

Clinton French, a private in my squad, went with me and helped me along. Coming to the first aide station (which was just two medical corpsmen with their field kit, located in a trench), French left me to return to the company. One of the medical corpsmen took my temperature saying it was 104 degrees. I spent the night here sleeping under a tree near the trench. At daylight two men came and helped me back to Chippy. Here they loaded me into an ambulance and we were soon on the shell-torn roads leading back from the front. After a long ride we came to Neufchatue, a town located in our old training area close to Gondrecaurt.

We unloaded and lined up with the many other men who were gassed and wounded on the front waiting for admission to the evacuation hospital. Many of them were so sick they were sitting about on the ground. I was almost unconscious from high temperature. Finally they took our names, etc., and assigned us to beds. The doctor, after a hasty examination, said I had influenza. They kept me here two days then put me aboard a train of boxcars with tiers of bunks in them. Inside were casualties from the combined French, American and German armies. There was a Frenchman in charge of our car and he sure was kept busy all the way to the base hospital which was our destination. After traveling for hours we pulled into the hospital center about thirty kilometers from Paris France.

They took me off the train, on a stretcher, to an influenza and pneumonia ward of Base Hospital No. 54. This hospital was so filled up with patients that they had to turn the recreation building into wards to take care of the steady stream of wounded and gassed men coming from the front. After I lay in bed for a few days I began to think I could get up and go about the hospital. But the nurse would not hear of it until a few days later she agreed to let me out of bed.

My clothes were brought to me and I began to put them on. I stood up beside the bed and then collapsed in a heap on the floor so weak I could not stand on my feet. I had to go back to bed for a few days longer. While in this ward I saw many men carried out, their fighting days over. Their places were soon filled with others coming in from the front.

We got news from the front daily from the Chicago Tribune which was published in Paris. In the latter part of October the papers were filled with news of a possible Armistice. The papers were selling at a premium for all that could walk went to a place a short distance from the hospital to buy a paper. Fighting was still going on at the front as the increasing number of patients indicated and on October 28th a trainload of us pulled out to return to the front.

In traveling in this manner an officer was placed in charge of traveling orders and transportation. We came to First Division where we went to a Red Cross canteen close to the railway station to get something to eat. Upon returning to the station a few minutes later we found our train had left out leaving many of us behind. Catching a later train, my buddy and I went on to Dijon in the same direction the other train had gone. Here we reported to the American railroad transportation office and requested transportation to our division. We were promptly arrested as stragglers and, under guard, we were sent to Es-Sur-Tiel about five kilometers away where they put us in a stockade prison.

We protested, of course, but it was useless for nothing was taken for granted. We stayed in this place for two days. At the end of this time a bunch of us loaded into a train and started again for our different organizations. We stopped at many places, finally on November 7th, coming up in back of the Argonne Front again. We camped here in billets in the woods that had been taken from the Germans. Thousands of American doughboys were in this replacement camp waiting to join their different organizations. It was anything but comfortable here in this sloppy, muddy place. With men from my own organization I made two attempts to rejoin my company but was told each time that the division was on a forced march on the city of Sedan at a great distance in the German lines and that it would be impossible.

MY EXPERIENCE IN THE GREAT WAR

ARMISTICE

The next morning we learned that the Armistice was signed. We celebrated with what we had at hand, with ammunition from the many ammunition dumps in the woods. Open fires were built now without any thought of enemy planes or observers seeing them and bombing or shelling our camps. There was no marked difference in the manner in which we were living. We continued on in camp here until a few days later all the men of the First Division as well as men from the many other divisions began marching toward Verdun to rejoin our different companies.

In this we were again disappointed for our outfit was too far ahead on the march to Germany for us to hope to catch up with them by hiking the only available means of transportation over the shell-torn battlefields. After moving from place to place about the former front we came to Don-Sur-Meuse about sixty kilometers north of Verdun. This place marked the end of the railroad leading into Germany and no rail traffic was possible until the railroad could be rebuilt. This was not completed until late in December. On January 5th, 1918 a trainload of us started for Germany. We traveled across the barren country that had seen so much of the hardest fighting of the war that it seemed as though it could

never be used as it was before the war began.
We passed on through this and into Germany glad of the opportunity to get away from the scenes of the battlegrounds. Crossing the Rhine River at Coblenz we went on to Montaban and the First Division Headquarters where we left the trains. I rejoined my company January 7, 1919 at Edysdorf in the Coblenz Bridge-Head area, about fourteen kilometers from Montaban. Other towns in which we were stationed during the following eight months were: Weroth, Nudenerbach, Hundsagin, Puttsbach, and a few weeks before we started for America we were stationed near the city of Neuweid. As the other American divisions left for home we took over their section of the "Neutral Zone line."
Finally the last of the American divisions left and it soon came our time to depart and on August 17th, 1919, we departed for Breast, France, and sailed for New York on August 23rd, arriving in New York September 2nd 1919. Those of us who had originally joined the First Division in Texas in 1917 had spent two years and three months in France and Germany and had been with the organization during the trying days at the front from November 1917 to the last time on the Argonne Front. I was with my company on the front six different times when we occupied the trenches in the Battlemont Sector, the Toul Sector, Catigny Sector, Port-A-Mausson Sector, St. Agnan Sector, and the Argonne Sector. After we paraded in New York Sept. 10th and Washington, D.C. Sept. 17th, 1919 we went to Camp Mead, Maryland where the "duration of the war" men were demobilized leaving just the regular army men who still had to serve out the rest of their three years actual army service and four years reserve. We moved from Camp Mead to Camp Taylor, Kentucky a few weeks later where we remained until I was discharged March 31, 1920 after serving in the army for a period of three years and one

MY EXPERIENCE IN THE GREAT WAR

month.

Eddie Anthony Sanders
Company K
26th Infantry
First US Division
 .

MY EXPERIENCE IN THE GREAT WAR

Le Bouret – France, March 24, 1919.

And I know another "Soldier"
Tho' she never shot [fired] a gun;
And she never seen the trenches
Or she never killed a Hun.
She's the Mother of that boy
I watched dying "over there"
She's a super-kind of soldier
For she gave more than her share;
She gave her country all she had,
Her pride, her love, her joy;
She's a splendid type of "soldier"
For she gave her "only boy"

MY EXPERIENCE IN THE GREAT WAR

EDDIE A. SANDERS

EDDIE A. SANDERS

MY EXPERIENCE IN THE GREAT WAR

EXTRACT FROM DISCHARGE CERTIFICATE OF ENLISTED MAN TO SECURE VICTORY MEDAL

This form will be prepared in accordance with the provisions of the Victory Medal Circular.

To all whom it may concern:

This is to certify, That Eddie A. Sanders 54746 Pvt. 1 cl. Co. K. 26th Inf., The United States Army, as a testimonial of honest and faithful service, is hereby Furloughed from the military service of the United States by reason of Cir. #78 WD 192.

Given under my hand at Camp Zachary Taylor, Ky. this

(Signed) William P. Martin
Col. 26th Infantry, Commanding.

ENLISTMENT RECORD

Enlisted, or inducted, Feb 22/ 1917, at Ft. Oglethorpe, Ga.

Battles, engagements, skirmishes, expeditions, Luneville Sec. 11/13-20/17; Toul Sec.3/7-4-9/18 Cantigny 5/27-30/18; Montdidier-Noyon 6/6-8/9/18 St. Mikiel 9/12-16/18.

Remarks: AWOL Aug 26-Sept 2/17; In absence under GO 31/12 or 45/16. Left US 6/14/17 arrived US 9/12/18.

(Signed) L. M. Jones, 2nd Lt. 26th Inf.
Commanding Co. K. 26th Inf.

Certificate to be made by a Civil Officer empowered to administer oaths or by an Officer of the Regular Army.

I certify that the foregoing is a true extract from the original discharge certificate (Form No. 525, A.G.O.) of Eddie A. Sanders 54746 Pvt. 1 cl. Co. K. 26th Inf., and contains all written and printed matter appearing on the discharge certificate opposite the headings hereon extracted, together with any notation or stamp with reference to a previous use of the discharge certificate for the purpose of obtaining Victory Medal.

I further certify that I have indorsed on the discharge certificate above my signature the following: "of Furlough, Regular Army Reserve certified by me on Aug 7/1920, 19____, for the purpose of obtaining Victory Medal only."

Place Army Recruiting Station, Atlanta, Ga.   Ed L. Baches
Date Aug 7/1920 [SEAL]   Joseph L. Baches, Capt. Inf. VMC

Form No. 745-2, A.G.O.

MY EXPERIENCE IN THE GREAT WAR

$8 A MONTH FOR DISABILITIES

MY EXPERIENCE IN THE GREAT WAR

EDDIE A. SANDERS (SEATED) AND
THE NORRIS BROTHERS

EDDIE A SANDERS

Made in the USA
Columbia, SC
26 September 2022